Sketches of Bromsgrove

by Bill Hazlehurst

Forty pen & ink sketches of
local buildings as they used to be
by the popular Midland artist

QuercuS

****
Quercus
John Roberts
8 Hillside Close, Bartley Green
Birmingham B32 4LT
****

Sketches of Bromsgove

by Bill Hazlehurst

ISBN 1 898136 09 2

First Published 1995

... publishing interesting books ...

Quercus is a regional publisher specialising in books about the West Midlands, Warwickshire, Worcestershire, Shropshire and south Staffs, with some some books on Wales.

We are interested in the region yesterday, today and tomorrow; in landscapes and trees, meadows and flowers, history, battles, lords and kings, castles and churches, bridges and tunnels. We want to know about industries and towns, people and customs, playgrounds and parks, myths and hauntings. We are interested in anything you find interesting.

Currently in print are *Midland Castles (£7.50), The Trackway of the Cross (£6.50), Sketches of Halesowen (£7.50), Midland Woods & rorests (£8.00), Midlands Ghosts & Hauntings (£6.00) Sketches of Birmingham (£8.00)* and *Australian Williams (£5.00)*.

Midland Woods & Forests was the first book in a series on the geography and natural history of the Midlands. *Midland Rivers* will be the second, to be followed by *Midland Lakes & Ponds*.

Midlands Parks, Midland Murders & Mysteries, Midland Country Houses (North), Coaching Days in the Midlands, Heart in my Boots and *Guide to Cotswold Villages* are all being written.

We are always willing to discuss ideas and proposals for new titles. If you have an idea but do not think you are up to writing about it, talk to us anyway. John Roberts might suggest a coauthorship arrangement in which you provided the research.

8 Hillside Close, Bartley Green, Birmingham
B32 4LT   0121 550 3158
(phone or write for further details)

Contents

The Artist

Bill Hazlehurst was born in Hockley, Birmingham in 1936, where his father was a policeman at Kenyon Street Police Station in the Jewellery Quarter and his mother a glass and silver worker. At Summer Lane Secondary School he had a good art teacher, a Miss Savage. His last school years involved two days a week at Vittoria Street Art School in the Jewellery Quarter learning silversmithing. Apart from this he is a self taught artist.

Starting work as a metal engraver, he switched at 19 to repairing mechanical accounting machines. Over the next thirty years he saw them replaced by electric models, then in turn, electronic valve, transistor and microchip machines. All the time Bill was retraining, and he was also sketching portraits of fellow engineers and machine operators.

Laurel and Hardy changed Bill's life in 1987 when, acting in a skit for charity he fell and smashed his ankle. Bored with idle time in hospital and at home in Hales Owen, Bill turned to his sketching. No human models were available, but an interest in the history of Hales Owen had turned up some old photos of the town. In this period Bill changed his technique from pencil to pen and ink.

Voluntary redundancy followed Bill's spell off work and he was able to develop a paying hobby into a business. Now he has a shop at Hagley Road, Hasbury, Hales Owen where he sells his own pictures and the work of other artists. Bill is married with two married daughters and two grandsons, and another grandchild due soon.

Photo: Glynnis Bateman

Bromsgrove

A range of small hills juts south from the Clent and Lickey Hills towards Redditch and Bromsgrove sits on their western flank. The salt road between Droitwich and the north passed through Bromsgrove and over the Lickeys, and although described as Roman, the line was probably prehistoric. The town is dominated by the hill on which St John's church stands and this was the focus of settlement. An Iron Age fort stood here but nothing remains except, perhaps, the ring of lime trees circling the churchyard. They have been replanted, generation after generation for countless centuries, and probably enclosed a pagan religious site with a oak at its centre.

In the 5th and 6th centuries the hill had a British (ie Celtic) settlement, and later a Saxon village. The Saxons built a wooden church to replace the oak tree. Their village was called at various times Bremesbyrig, Bremesgrefa and Bremsgrave, and is recorded in the Domesday Survey of 1086 as having three (water) mills and 18 villages within its manor.

Bromsgrove was a Royal Manor held directly by the king, and this was the case until Henry VIII granted it in succession to several of his wives. Elizabeth I gave it to the Earl of Warwick in 1564, but in 1604 it came back again, so James I gave it to Sir Richard Grobham. It was willed or sold in turn to the Howe family and the Earl of Plymouth, and remained with them until 1947. The manor was then bought by Mr Howard Bird, and Bromsgrove still has a Lord of the Manor in Mr Christopher Bird. However modern laws have reduced the rights to no more than a title, probably to the relief of local farmers and maidens.

Bromsgrove retains a ceremonial survival of the feudal system in the Court Leet, or Court of the Lord of the Manor. This was the medieval form of local government, with reeves, beedles, affeerors and all sorts of folk. It still meets every spring and autumn to appoint its officers and adjudicate on offences, such as throwing slops and singeing pigs in the High Street.

Bromsgrove was at the meeting of roads to Worcester, Birmingham, Kidderminster, Coventry and Stratford upon Avon, making it a centre for trade. At one time there were 59 inns. King John granted a Charter in 1199 permitting a weekly market on Tuesdays and annual fairs on 25th June and 29th August. Edward I granted the privilege of sending two members of Parliament but the citizens asked to be relieved of the expense.

From the late middle ages the town's crafts developed into industries. Bromsgrove had water power from the vigorous little streams off the Lickey Hills and by 1800 there were some 20 mills. As the economy shifted from agriculture to manufacture they converted from grinding grain to cotton, needle, saw, fulling, tanning, paper and whitesmithing mills. Coal and iron were at hand to the north, so with much of the Black Country, nail making developed as a cottage industry with each house having its forge. Organised by merchants who put out work and bought the nails, the trade dominated the town and satellite villages. It paid badly, the hours were long and the work exhausting, but it continued from the early 16th century into the 20th.

In the 19th century Bromsgrove was described as; "..... *a large but dirty place, full of shops and manufacturers of nails, needles and some .... coarse linens.*" This comes from *Beauties of England and Wales,* making either the title or the reference to Bromsgrove rather odd.

Salt was extracted at Stoke Prior from 1825 and was used to make alkali, sulphuric acid and soap. The wells flooded in 1850 and ruined some firms, but they were restored and the saltworks became the biggest in the world. It closed in 1972.

Bromgsrove Guild of Applied Arts was formed as part of the late 19th century Arts and Crafts movement. Starting with the promotion of furniture making, it extended to metal working and stained glass. The Guild obtained the contract to make the gates and railings of Buckingham Palace, which so increased its stature that orders poured in. Craftsmen were recruited from many corners of Europe and the Guild sent fabulous iron gates, stained glass and woodwork all over the world. World War I dispersed the workforce, distorted the world economy and destroyed the market for artistic works. The Guild was reformed in 1921 and survived in much reduced form until 1966. A local example of the Guild's work is a set of gates in All Saints church and there are others in the Museum.

After World War II and before the decades of redevelopment in the 1960's and 70's, Bromsgrove found itself with a huge range and variety of buildings. There was medieval timber framing, georgian brick, the whole gamut of Victorian architecture from stucco to romantic pointy gables, a sample of mild art deco from the 1930's and the ubiquitous Queen Anne Post Office. But as the old photos show, many of these buildings were in poor repair, inconvenient or unsuitable for modern needs, and perhaps not terribly interesting. Whatever people think about that, most of the modern replacements are much less interesting, and often too high, too flat or too boringly featureless. Fortunately for Bromsgrove, there remains a lively variety and a friendly jumble with plenty of interest.

The Sketches

The pictures are mixed into no particular scheme, though some connected views are in sequence. The emphasis is on the older buildings, many of which no longer exist, so you may find some pictures difficult to recognise. The views are from different periods because Bill's drawings come from whatever sources are available, photos of varying quality taken over more than a hundred years supported by research and his own recollections and observations.

This is not a complete collection of all Bromsgrove's historic or interesting buildings, that would have taken another volume or so, we have had to select. Nor is it a detailed history of the town or an architectural analysis of its buildings, and the notes about each picture are brief. We have written them assuming that they might be read by newcomers and visitors to Bromsgrove, so if we say things that you know very well, bear with us.

We have drawn on many sources for the pictures and information. Thanks to the anonymous photographers who left their records of the town, and patient local historians who have assembled coherent histories from all the fragments. There are two comprehensive and authoritative books which we found valuable and must acknowledge and recommend.

Bromsgrove Now and Then by Alan and Sheila Richards, (The Bromsgrove Society. ISBN 0 9509471 3 X - £9.50)

The Bromsgrove Time Machine by Alan Richards and Norman Neesom (Broomhill Press - £6.75.)

Finally, Bill would like to thank Barry T Carpenter of Mis Print, High Street, Bromsgrove for his help in producing this book.

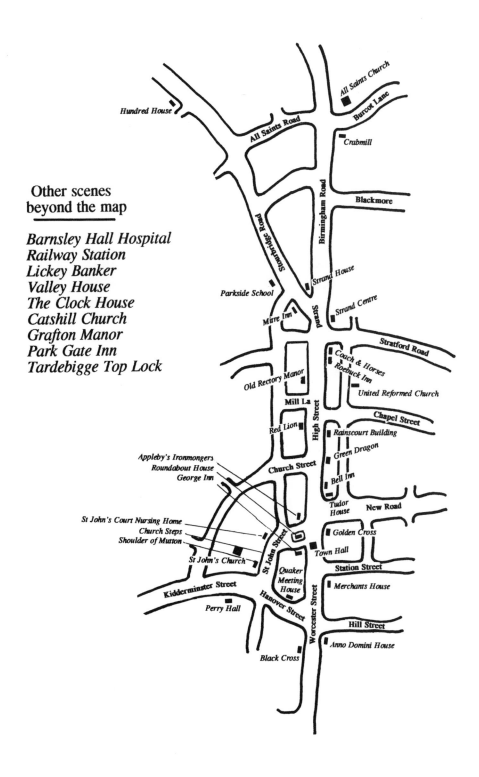

Other scenes
beyond the map

Barnsley Hall Hospital
Railway Station
Lickey Banker
Valley House
The Clock House
Catshill Church
Grafton Manor
Park Gate Inn
Tardebigge Top Lock

Hundred House

All Saints Church

Burcot Lane

All Saints Road

Birmingham Road

Crabmill

Blackmore

Strand House

Stourbridge Road

Strand

Strand Centre

Parkside School

Mitre Inn

Stratford Road

Coach & Horses

Roebuck Inn

Old Rectory Manor

United Reformed Church

Mill La

High Street

Chapel Street

Red Lion

Rainscourt Building

Green Dragon

Appleby's Ironmongers
Roundabout House
George Inn

Church Street

Bell Inn

Tudor House

New Road

St John's Court Nursing Home
Church Steps
Shoulder of Mutton

St John Street

Golden Cross

Town Hall

St John's Church

Quaker Meeting House

Worcester Street

Station Street

Kidderminster Street

Merchants House

Hanover Street

Perry Hall

Hill Street

Anno Domini House

Black Cross

1. Anno Domini House

This attractive old timber framed building stood
at the junction of Hill Lane and Worcester Street
opposite Kidderminster Road. The name arose from
half a mill wheel fixed over the end door bearing
the date 1581 with the words *ANNO DOM* on each
side. We know the wheel was fixed by Mr Wildsmith,
Furniture Broker, who owned the house in the 19th
century, but not why. It was certainly one of the
oldest houses in the town and had once been the
Black & White Inn.

Anno Domini House, Worcester St. Bromsgrove.

St. John's, Bromsgrove.

2. St John's Church

High on its sandstone hill and ringed by tall lime trees, this is one of the great churches of the Midlands. The 198 foot red spire is soaringly impressive from all angles, and the body of the church spreads itself comfortably over the churchyard.

St John's stands on the site of a wooden saxon church, and there is some evidence that it was pagan site. It may well have been an Iron Age fort on the salt road from Droitwich and to the Lickey Hills and the north.

The first stone church was Norman from the reign of Henry II. Very little of that remains but there is 13th century work; the tower and spire are 14th century. A great deal of what you now see is the result of restoration in 1858 by the eminent church architect Sir George Gilbert Scott. There are ten bells and the oldest was cast in 1701.

The clock was installed in 1684, the chimes came later in 1775 but they no longer work. In 1860 it was moved from the tower to the spire so as to be more visible and useful to the town.

3. Old Town Hall & Market

Bromsgrove's first Town Hall, or Market Hall, was a timber framed Elizabethan structure, not unlike the one still standing at Ledbury. This was replaced in 1832 by the brick and stone building pictured, which was financed by a loan from the wealthy men of the town.

The Board, or Town Council, met in the upper floor until the building was demolished in 1928.

The market stalls stood in the open at the front and at back of the Hall, much as they had done since the Middle Ages. Until 1926 they reached up the High Street from the Town Hall to the Crescent, and all shops and houses on the street had the right to one.

Old Town Hall and Market, Bromsgrove.

(11)

"The Red Lion" High St, Bromsgrove.

4. Red Lion

The Red Lion is still there and shares this old
building with Blunts shoe shop. Until late in the
19th century it was the dignified Georgian home
of Doctor Joseph Horton. The buildings on either
side illustrate the mixture which is Bromsgrove.
On the near side we have timber framing and on
the other a gabled Victorian building. With its
weathered bricks and battered porch, the Red
Lion has not changed much over the years.

5. The Bell Inn

This pub stood at No 60 High Street. It was once known as the Lower Dolphin and before that, the White Swan. The Upper Dolphin was at the top (Birmingham) end of the High Street. It became the Bell in 1771 when renamed by its proprietor, Mr Willam Rose, who was Parish Clerk and a bellringer.

During demolition in 1964 the contractors found that the Georgian style frontage had been applied to a 16th century timber framed house, which was not at all unusual.

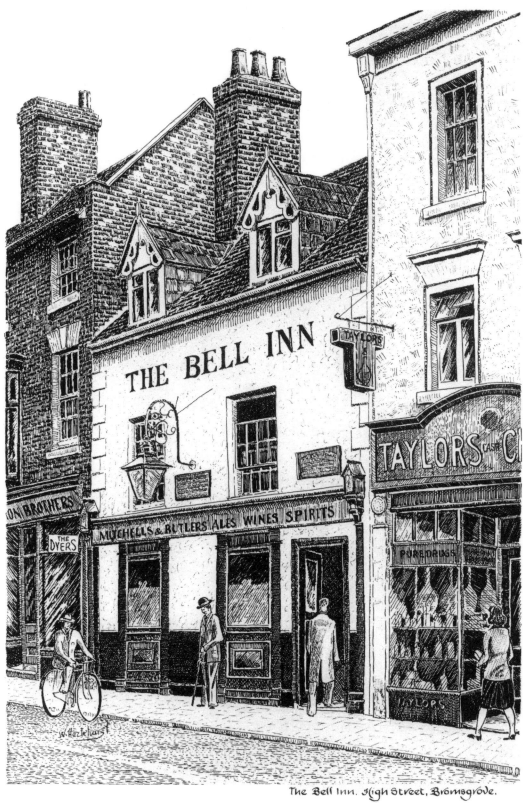

The Bell Inn. High Street, Bromsgrove.

Coach & Horses, High Street, Bromsgrove.

6. Coach & Horses

This old inn survived until recently, sort of. The original building stood next to the Roebuck at the junction of High Street and Stratford Road. Both were coaching inns, with a coach entrance to the Roebuck on Stratford Road and that for the Coach & Horses under the attractive gabled window in the picture. The Roebuck was the posting house for the mail from London to Wolverhampton.

In the 1970's most of the site became the square, blocky Kwik-Save supermarket, with a featureless brick box stuck on the side for the pub. This has now become an American pool hall called "The Hustler", after the famous Paul Newman film.

7. The Old Rectory Manor

Rectory Manor House was one of the oldest stone buildings in Bromsgrove and stood in the High Street near Mill Lane. It was occupied for many years by Mr F Watton, Undertaker, who also ran a coach and cab company. He was one of several Wattons in business along the High Street.

The Manor was part of the ancient Forest of Feckenham and before the Reformation had been granted to St Mary's Monastery Church at Worcester The Prior of Worcester Convent held a court in the house twice a year. By the 19th century the Manor belonged to the Dean and Chapter of Worcester Cathedral who leased the house to the Windsor family of Hewell Grange. Much of the land was used in the 1840's as a racecourse which ran from Church Street to Parkside School playing fields.

Bryant's Garage (visible in the sketch) bought the building in 1921 for use as a showroom, and it was demolished. The rest of the buildings disappeared during the building of Mill Street Precinct.

The Old Rectory Manor, High Street, Bromsgrove.

(19)

The Strand, Bromeqrove.

8. The Strand

The Mitre Inn on the left of the sketch was one of many timber framed buildings encased in brick in the Georgian period. It still stands and timbers are visible at the back. The pub was once Bromsgrove's centre for cider making but is now offices.

Outside the picture on the left, a row of shops or offices has been inserted between the Queens Head and the Mitre. This was the site of the bus station, and before that, the Bell Foundry.

Strand House in the centre of the picture was originally known as the Cock Hall. Bromsgrove Parish acquired it in 1723 and the building was enlarged and converted into the town's first workhouse. In 1838 another was built near All Saints church and this building became a tannery.

An account of The Strand in the 1860's mentions that in road in front of the tannery was a small, hexagonal, single storey building called "the round house". It was the office for the public weighbridge which was let into the road between the two buildings. We do not know when it was removed.

The Strand is a name found in many places and means a margin of land on the banks of a river. The Spadesbourne Brook crosses the top of the High Street in a culvert. The dip in the road may be evidence that there was once a ford.

9. The Merchant's House

This quaint, timber framed building stood at the corner of Worcester Street and Station Street. It was built around 1450 for a wealthy wool merchant and later belonged to a succession of prosperous clothiers and dyers.

It is the only large house in Bromsgrove to have survived from the Middle Ages, though with the inevitable extensions and alterations. The old Hop Pole in New Street and the Rainscourt Building (sketches 17 and 37) are about a century later.

The oak frame is fixed by wooden pegs and the panels are wattle and daub; most later timber framed buildings in the Midlands have brick infill. The arrangements were typical of the medieval hall house. Front and back doors opened into a cross passage which divided the living area from the cooking and storage rooms. Originally the ground floor rooms were open to the roof.

The old house was demolished in 1962 but the timbers were taken to Avoncroft College for storage. It was gradually restored to resemble as far as possible its appearance when built, and in 1967 became the first exhibit of the Avoncroft Museum.

The Merchant's House, Bromsgrove.

Green Dragon. High St., Bromsgrove.

10. Green Dragon

In the 1960's Boots the Chemist was extended to cover the site of the Green Dragon. During the 1850's the licensee was a Mr Munslow and he held a weekly pig market on Tuesdays in the pub yard. The Green Dragon and The Bell were the pubs where were local Friendly Societies held their annual dinners on Whit Monday, before marching to St John's church in the wake of a military band.

11. Black Cross

The Black Cross at the junction of Hill Street, Worcester Street and Hanover Street was built in the early 17th century. It is Bromsgrove's oldest pub and was fully restored in 1985. The upper storey is timber framed and the lower one was originally sandstone, but has been rebuilt in brick.

Charles II probably called at the smithy attached to the Black Cross in 1651. After his defeat at the Battle of Worcester the King made his way discreetly to Shropshire, then returned south disguised as the servant of Jane Lane, sister of his loyal officer, Colonel Lane. Near Bromsgove the horse they were riding cast a shoe. Charles later told the diarist Samuel Pepys how he held the horses leg for the smith and asked the news. The smith reported that the Scots had been defeated, which was good news, but the rogue Charles Stuart had escaped. Charles replied that if he were taken he deserved to be hanged more than all the rest.

The name Black Cross is not common and may come from the old custom of burying evildoers at a crossroads, which is where the pub stands, rather than in hallowed ground. The cross on the sign is Maltese which might suggest some connection with the Knights of St John who owned Malta between the 16th and the 18th centuries. (It is the emblem of St John's Ambulance.) However this may be an artistic flourish by a more modern sign painter since a photo of 1885 shows a cross more like the sails of a windmill, which is not dissimilar but has no nicks in the arms. In fact this cross may have prompted the suggestion of a link with the north European Tutonic Knights, whose symbol was the iron cross. Goodness knows what they would have been doing in Bromsgrove; perhaps the later artist was right, since we have at least a church of St John.

Black Cross, Bromsgrove.

Bromsgrove Railway Station.

12. Railway Station

The sketch shows a view from the station approach across the forecourt to the "up" building, with its twin porticos. The signal box is out of view to the right but can be seen in drawing 13 - The Lickey Banker. Bromsgrove was a First Class station, and when it was opened housed the offices of the Secretary and Resident Engineer of the Birmingham & Gloucester Railway that built the line. These buildings have all gone, leaving only the platforms adorned by two bus shelters.

Two headstones stand side by side in St John's churchyard to Thomas Scaife and Joseph Rutherford. These engine drivers died at the station in 1840 when their boiler exploded. The locomotive pictured is an unusual 4-2-0, and perhaps some railway expert can tell us whether it was one of the Norris's imported from Philadelphia to assist trains up the Lickey Bank.

13. The Lickey Banker

The Midland Railway never ran trains heavier than they needed to be but offered frequent services. Consequently their locomotives tended to be light, and double heading of trains was common.

With the Birmingham & Gloucester Railway's main line, the Midland took on the longest steepest, main line gradient in Britain, the Lickey Bank between Bromsgove and Birmingham at 1 in 37. In the early years the Midland imported special engines from the USA, later goods trains were pushed up the incline by up to four extra engines at the back. The eventual answer was the monster four cylinder 0-10-0 in the picture built at the Midlands' Derby works in 1919, the biggest thing they ever made.

Big Emma or *Big Bertha* as she was called, had two identical boilers which were used alternately, one in use, the other being repaired. Her great power meant that she could both haul the trains and apply steam braking on all ten wheels.

During 1924 she was transferred to the London main lines to haul coal trains, but she was built for high power over short distances, did not perform well and was soon returned to Bromsgrove. She carried various numbers, of which the best known was 2290. After 1923 when the Midland became part of the LMS she became 22290, and under British Rail 58100. In the last days of steam her work was done by the most powerful locomotive ever to run in Britain, a massive six cylinder Garratt.

The Lickey Banker

St. John Street, Bromsgrove.

(32)

14. St John Street

This timber framed building now which is occupied by the Birmingham Midshires Building Society once had more gables. A bay in the High Street vanished in 1898 when Manchester House was built, and a couple more round the corner in St John Street were demolished in 1960 when the Society re-built the corner. The ornamental late 16th century timberwork over Appleby's Ironmongers shop shop was plastered over in the early 19th century and not seen again until 1910.

The modern office front is not unsympathetic to the uneven, slightly battered timberwork and humpy clay tiled roof, but the flat roof beside it is simply savage.

The sketch shows the old mens' toilets which were built right over the Spadesbourne Brook, but not the George Hotel. Sketch 15 - Roundabout House is a view in the opposite direction.

15. Roundabout House

This old building stood next to the Town Hall in St John's Street and on the corner opposite to the Birmingham Midshires building. At one time it was a mill and was also known as Roundabout Mill. There was only the narrow passage in the picture between it and the shops opposite. They were timber framed buildings but covered in stucco in the early 19th century. Latter it was the warehouse of William Llewellyn, corn merchant, maltster and hop dealer. Roundabout House was demolished in 1898 and the other buildings in the 1960's.

The bridge in the foreground over the Spadesbourne Brook was built in 1830. Before that vehicles drove through the water and pedestrians crossed by a plank footbridge which had been built in 1755 by the Church Wardens. On Friday 13th March 1792 the river flooded and the depth was recorded on Roundabout House at 5 feet above the street.

Bridge and the Roundabout House, St. John St., Bromsgrove c.1890

(35)

Hanover Street. Bromsgrove.

16. Hanover Street

Hanover Street exits in name but all these buildings have been demolished since the 1960's. Only No 1 remains but is beyond the left side of the picture. It was one of the most interesting streets in the town.

In the 18th century there were several weaving shops, probably because they were near to the cotton mill in Watts Close and Sideamoor Mill, which spun linen yarn.

The timber framed building on the right was most probably a private house in the 16th century but became a Quaker Meeting House from about 1700.

Hanover House on the left was a school in the 1850's with a part in use as a chapel. A cottage beside it was unchanged for many years and was still using a black iron grate for coal fines in 1987.

17. Hop Pole

The Hop Pole in New Road was a coaching inn which survived by a small miracle and forms an unusual early example of conservation.

It was built on the High Street in 1572, rather early for such elaborate timber framing and sumptuously decorated woodwork, but read on. In 1840 the new railway was opened and it soon became obvious that narrow, steep Station Road was inadequate. The Hop Pole was to be demolished to create New Road.

There was no legal protection for valued buildings in those days. The endless cheerful demolition and rebuilding by the Victorians demonstrates their vigorous self confidence and some indifference to preserving the past that was widely questioned only at the end of the century. However people from within Bromsgrove and outside stopped total destruction of the Hop Pole and preserved all the main components.

In 1866/7 it was rebuilt in New Road by the builder who had demolished it, adding some new timbers and carving by local craftsmen. In 1868 it was re-opened as a bank and is now known as Tudor House.

The commanding central bay with its porch are flanked by two supporting wings. The barge boards are carved with grape vines, scollops, flowers, leaves, serpents and dragons and there are lots of fine nobbles and twiddles on the gable finials. See if you can spot the Victoriana in all this.

The rebuilt 'Hop Pole', New Road, Bromsgrove.

(39)

The Church Steps, Bromsgrove.

(40)

18. Church Steps

To climb the long flight of worn sandstone steps to the lychgate and to come upon St John's is to slip into the past. The fine lychgate was built in 1656 during the rule of Oliver Cromwell. Every town needs these charming retreats.

The original 62 steps have now been reduced to 48, possibly because of a rise in the surface of St John's Street below by continual resurfacing.

19. Barnsley Hall Hospital

This is the back of the former mental hospital which was built in 1903, straightforwardly classical and businesslike. The front had some mildly frivolous gables. But the most mundane and practical structure, the water tower, has been turned into a madly romantic gingerbread fairy castle. Water was pumped from two 360 foot boreholes making the hospital self suffient.

Weeds and scrub have invaded the grounds and the fences are broken down. We no longer need many of these big places because patients are generally treated in the community. A proposal to demolish the hospital and build a shopping centre was refused planning permission and its future is uncertain.

The land was part of the Barnsley Hall Estate but the Hall itself was pulled down in 1769. A big farmhouse was built nearby and is still called Barnsley Hall Farm.

Barnsley Hall Hospital, Bromsgrove.

(43)

All Saints, Bromsgrove.

20. All Saint's Church

This big church in Birmingham Road was designed
by the architect John Cotton and built in 1874. The
original plans included a steeple but there were some
doubts about the foundations and a tower was added
in 1888. This might explain the surprised look of
its lancet windows. The apse and trancepts give the
church a massive and slightly continental appearance. It is built of brick clad with pale sandstone
which is weathering, but less than the local red
sandstone.

If you like high Victorian churches, try to get a look
at the interior. The Vicar, John Cook is a friendly
chap and quite enthusiastic about his church. The
wide and lofty nave has pale brick walls patterned
with bricks of other colours. There is a fair amount
of stained glass, mostly Victorian but some from
the 1920's and later, and it generally seems of
good quality. The organ is an unusual one for an
English church, a Italian make which is modern
but built to classical Italian designs.

21. The Crabmill

Entering Bromsgrove from the Birmingham direction, the Crabmill on the corner of Birmingham Road and Burcot Lane is a very handsome 18th century building The generously proportioned Venetian style windows and classical doorway look genially welcoming and show how plain designs can be decorative. In 1778 the Crabmill was described as *"a noted inn"*.

The Spadesbourne Brook runs very close to the inn and most likely powered the landlord's cider press.

The Crabmill, Bromsgrove.

(47)

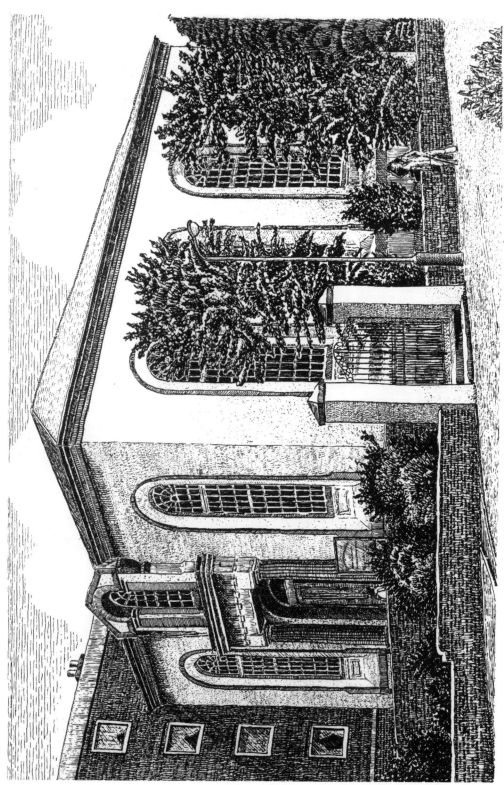

Bromsgrove United Reform Church.

22. United Reformed Church

On this site which is now in Chapel Street stood
the farm of Nicholas Blick which was used in the
17th century as a Prebyterian Meeting House. It was
one of four Bromsgrove houses which could be used
for religious purpose under the Toleration Act of
1689. Two barns at the back were later converted
into a chapel for an annual rent of one red rose.

In 1692 John Spilsbury, son of a puritan Vicar of
St John's in 1650's, bought land to the rear and
built Bromsgrove's first Independent Chapel. This
later became the Congregation Church and is now
the United Reformed Church.

This present stucco building was built in 1833 by
the Congregationalists. The massive porch lintel
and upper window are supported on rather spindly
doric columns, but the whole thing seems seriously
solid and worthy.

23. Old Market Place

In 1199 King John granted Bromsgrove the right to hold a market every Tuesday and annual fairs on 24th June and 29th August. For centuries the busiest part of town was the junction of St John Street and High Street where Roundabout House (or Mill) stood very close to the old Market Hall.

The timber framed building on the corner appears from a slightly different angle in sketch 14 - St John Street, where we commented on the lost gables. It was probably the site of the first Golden Cross Inn.

The Market Place today is a small remnant of what it used to be when stalls would reach from here up the High Street to the Crescent at the far end. The smart new Market Hall in St John Street continues an 800 year tradition.

Old Market Place. Bromsgrove.

Housman Statue, High St., Bromsgrove.

(52)

24. Housman Statue

This rough hewn statue of the poet by Kenneth Potts has stood in the High Street since 1983. Only the rather miserable looking hat crumpled against his stick lightens the figure of this sombre, unhappy man. An inscription on the plinth quotes from Housman's sequel of poems *A Shropshire Lad*.

> *"and brooding on my heavy ill,*
> *I met a statue standing still."*

The Housman family lived at the Clock House, Fockbury, near Catshill and during the 1870's he walked daily to Bromsgrove School.

Much of his curiously disturbing poetry was written here before Housman had ever set foot in Shropshire. However he had seen the hills from Worms Ash near his home, and for him it was less a real place than a mythical land of lost content. His poems, full of the pain of loss and longing, have been described as the poetry of despair. He was a strong influence on the slightly later "georgian pastoralist" group of English composers. Three of them, Ivor Gurney, George Butterworth and Vaughan Williams, set *A Shropshire Lad* as a song cycle.

25. Valley House

A E Housman was born in this house at Fockbury on 26th March 1859, the son of Edward and Sarah Jane Williams. He was christened by his Grand-father, the Reverend Thomas Housman, in Catshill church the following Easter Sunday. The family lived only one year at Valley House before moving to Perry Hall.

After the Housmans left Valley House became a Dame's school run by the Misses Bradley. By 1938 it belonged to Miss Isobel Morcom who renamed it *"Housman's"*. At about this time the porch was added and the building converted from a farm house to a comfortable residence.

Valley House (Housmans), Fockbury.

Davey Hall. Bromsgrove

(56)

26. Perry Hall

Shortly after A E Housman was born, Perry Hall fell vacant on the death of Captain John Adams at the age of 91. Captain Adams was Edward Housman's great uncle with whom he worked in a solicitors practice, and had built the house in 1824.

The Hall was built from the ruins of an older house of the same name, and an ivy covered wall of the 17th century building can still be seen.

Edward Housman planted a chestnut tree for young Alfred and later one for each of his children. There is a story that when he was at work but wanted a drink, he would lob a stone onto the tin roof of an outhouse. The landlord of the Leg of Mutton would hear it a bring a jug of ale.

In 1872 when Alfred was 12, financial pressures compelled the family to give it up and move to the Clock House at Fockbury.

The Hall is now a hotel. Although it was built in 1824 in the 18th century style, the windows show the influence of gothic romanticism which was to have such an effect on Victorian buildings from churches to gasworks and railway stations.

27. The Clock House

The Housman family's move from Perry Hall to the Clock House at Fockbury in 1872 was not an easy one. Their new home had no gas, water or main drainage. However for a child it was a magical place with a big garden, orchards, barns, stables, lofts and cartsheds.

The Clock House came to Joseph Brettle through his marriage to Ann Holden in 1782, and their daughter married the Reverend Thomas Housman, A E's grandfather who was Vicar of Kinver. He moved into the Clock House in 1838 when he became the Vicar of Catshill, and lived there until he died in 1872.

The name of the house came from a big clock in one of the gables. It was removed to allow for extensions to accommodate the growing Housman family, and from this time the name became Fockbury House. It was demolished in the 1960's and the only "remains" are bogus, an overgrown red brick tower and clock built in the 1920's. The sketch shows an amiably rambling, timber framed house, probably built towards the end of the period of timber construction.

The Clock House, Fockbury.

Christ Church, Catshill

28. Christ Church, Catshill

Christ Church was built in 1838. The red sandstone is mellow and friendly but very badly weathered. In fact the tower is currently fenced off to protect people from flying chunks. The design is run of the mill Victorian.

A E Housman's grandfather, the Reverend Thomas, Housman became the first Vicar. Several Housman relatives were buried here, the Reverend Thomas, and Alfred's father Edward, mother Sarah and step mother, Lucy.

When the Housman's left Perry Hall for the Clock House in 1872 the chestnut trees which Edward had planted for each child were lifted and planted around the churchyard. Some survive.

29. Shoulder of Mutton

This pub still stands in St John's Street under the church but has been given a modern timber board frontage. That was only the latest transformation because the Shoulder of Mutton is one of the town's oldest pubs. It was built in 1610 as a coaching inn but largely rebuilt in the late 19th century. This accounts for the pleasant brick arches over the windows and door.

John Pugh in his interesting book *Bromsgrove and the Housmans* says he was told that caves exist in the sandstone cliff behind the inn where monks did their penances. Quite recently a new landlord was clearing his garden when he came upon two openings which might be the same. The pub is supposed to be haunted by a cloak wearing ghost.

Legend has it that a tunnel ran from the Shoulder of Mutton to Grafton Manor but no trace of it has been found. Given that the distance is nearly a mile and a quarter it seems an unlikely medieval engineering feat.

'Shoulder of Mutton', St. John St. Bromsgrove.

Grafton Manor, Bromsgrove.

30. Grafton Manor I

Grafton Manor stands at the end of a lane near the M5, about a mile and a half south of the town. Two of the great English families have lived here, the Staffords and the Talbots, and both were heavily involved in English history.

After the Battle of Hastings the land was granted to Urso d'Abitor, a cousin of William I. It belonged to the Graftons from the reign of Henry I to Edward I, to the Warwickshire Hastings family up to the middle of the 13th century, and then passed by marriage to the Staffords. Sir Humphrey Stafford was Lord of the Manor of Grafton in 1450. He was very close to Henry VI and a soldier of high reputation who was killed in Jack Cades's Kentish rebellion in that year.

A second Sir Humphrey, nephew of the above, supported Richard III at the Battle of Bosworth in 1585. This was most unfortunate because the victor was the Welshman, Henry Tudor - Henry IV. He awarded the Manor of Grafton to Sir Gilbert Talbot of Shropshire who had played an important part in the battle. Stafford escaped but was later caught and hanged. The Manor remained in the Talbot family until 1935.

We have no idea what the medieval house looked like, but it was rebuilt in the Tudor style of 1567. The diaper patterned brickwork, crow stepped gables and clusters of chimneys you see today follow restoration after a great fire in 1710, but must resemble the original. The porch and gable pictured survived the fire but the porch has the classical touches of the early 17th century, so might have been a later embellishment.

On a plaque over the gable window is inscribed:

> *"Plieti and grase*
> *Bi in this place*
> *Whyle every man is pleased in his degree*
> *There is both peace and unity*
> *Salaman saith there's none accorde*
> *When every man would be a lord."*

31. Grafton Manor II

Grafton Manor today is a fine hotel and the present owner, John Morris, has done much to restore the old building to its former glory.

The lawns are arranged in three tiers with steps between leading down to a lake. By the water stands a derelict dovecote which had largely deteriorated during this century. Within one of the lawns is a fish stew, or pond to keep fish after they had been caught in the lake. The dovecote and the stew provided fresh eggs, meat and fish throughout the year. This might appeal to people staying at the hotel, but Mr Morris has thought it best to drain the pond and make it safe for children. However, it will not just be filled and lost, but converted into a sunken garden

Grafton Manor. Bromsgrove.

(67)

Park Gate Inn, Kidderminster Road, Bromsgrove.

32. Park Gate Inn

The Park Gate Inn is about a mile and a half from
town and just off the Kidderminster road. It is an
old place and one wonders how it came to be here.
The name suggests an entrance to the park of Grafton
Manor; nearby we have Park Farm, a quarter mile off
Warridge Lodge Farm, further south are South Lodge
and West Lodge Farms, then on the edge of the town
are East Lodge and Park Hall.

33. The Hundred House

The Hundred House is shown here as the inn that it was, but the old building on Stourbridge Road has long been converted to apartments. The exterior is not much changed, the attractive gables, porch bay windows and oriel window over the main road all remain, but the brickwork has been rendered.

Before the Norman Conquest civil administration was based on the Shire and a subdivision of it, the Hundred. Bromsgrove was originally in the Hundred of Worces- tershire. Later it was joined with Clent to form the Hundreds of Halfshire. It is likely that the Courts of Halfshire were held near to the site of the Hundred House.

The Hundred House, Stourbridge Road Bromsgrove.

(71)

Tardebigge Top Lock. Worcester & Birmingham Canal.

(72)

34. Tardebigge Top Lock

The Birmingham & Worcester Canal was difficult.
It was authorised by an Act of Parliament of 1791,
but problems of water supply and the colossal Wast
Hill Tunnel delayed the work. By 1807 boats could
reach Tardebigge, but here the canal stopped for
some years while the Company considered how to
save money on the descent to the Severn plain.
Work was not completed until 1818.

There are no locks between the northern terminus at
Gas Street, Birmingham and Tardebigge because the
engineers could build embankments, cuttings and
tunnels to avoid changes of level. But in the two
and a half miles between Tardebigge to Stoke Prior
there is a fall of 259 feet which now involves 35
locks. (The Tardebigge Flight as such has 29 of
them.) This was the eventual solution, but for a
period a boat lift worked in place of the Top Lock,
which explains its unusual depth of 14 feet.

On the Birmingham side of the Top Lock is a tunnel
about a third of a mile long. There was no towpath
so boats were legged through by men lying on their
backs and "walking" along the tunnel lining. Many
lives were lost in this dangerous business and steam
tugs were used from 1874.

Bromsgrove is a mile from its railway station but
two and a half miles from the canal, so goods went
to and from Tardebigge and Stoke wharfs by cart.

The B&W Canal is one of the most attractive in the
Midlands - go and have an amble along the towpath.
The picture includes a distant view of the fairyland
spire of Tardebigge Church on its commanding hill.
Tardebigge is a Saxon name meaning the tower on
the hill.

35. St John's Court
Nursing Home

You can see that the oldest part of this building is the projecting central block. The rather serious looking dutch style gables and the tiny cylindrical oriel window were designed in 1848 for the Vicarage of St John's church. The Urban District Council took it over and built the extensions as offices when they moved from the old Town Hall. When the Council moved once more the building became the nursing home, and seems appropriately restful.

St Johns Court Nursing Home, Bromsgrove.

The Strand, Bromsgrove.

(76)

36. The Strand

Once called The Crescent, this wide street with its
slight curve has the potential to be a very pleasant
and imposing public space. We say it has potential
because at present it is cluttered and marred by
traffic. We say imposing because it has a greater
proportion of buildings with character than most
sections of the High Street and is a rather more
interesting shape.

These buildings are not much altered though their
uses have changed. In the commentary on the other
sketch of The Strand - 8, we mentioned the old
tannery which is now Strand House, also not much
altered. The main change to the structures has been
in the buildings opposite those in this sketch. A
row of offices now fits well between the Queens
Head and an office building which used to be the
Mitre. These buildings replaced the bus station,
which replaced a foundry, and represent scenic
improvement - except to people who like buses
and foundries.

37. Rainscourt Building

This complete timber framed house was built in the late 16th century. The close spacing of the timbers indicates some wealth and it was probably built by a wealth cloth merchant. They also suggest a fairly late date in the period of timber building.

We know that for many years the left side was the Unicorn Inn but this probably closed in the 1850's. At that time the right side was occupied by J Lacy - Tailor. It has probably seen many trades.

The upper storey timbers and windows were restored in 1987, the new work has not yet weathered and is quite obvious. There are attractive details on the gable peaks and decorated brackets under the third storey windows. This homely old building seems rather dowdy beside the prosperous windows and ample proportions of Lloyd's Bank.

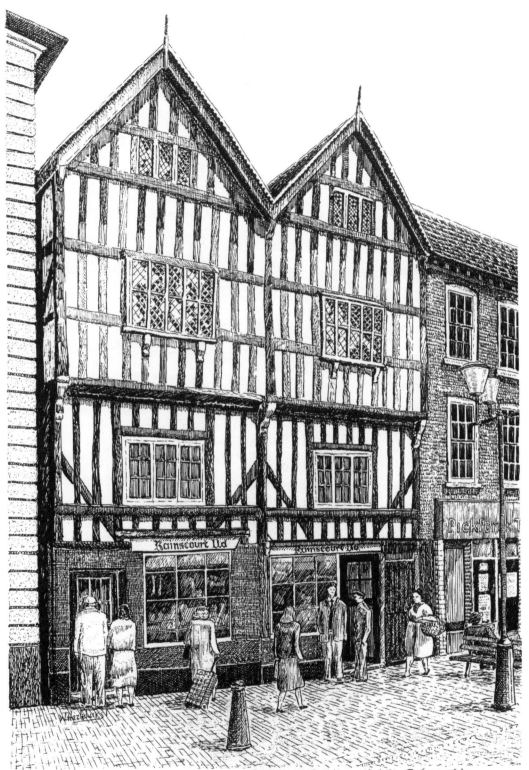

Rainscourt Building   High St, Bromsgrove.

High Street Precinct, Bromsgrove.

38. High Street Precinct

There are a lot of crass or merely undistinguished modern buildings in the High Street, but the mixture with the older ones that remain creates a lively variety. The car-free section is now tree lined and well lit on winter nights and redeems nearly everything. It has created a very pleasant street which the people of Bromsgrove can use and enjoy; traders like it and motorists - well they are pedestrians as well. Like all such schemes, it drives an appetite for more.

39. High Street

This is a modern view from the site of the old George Hotel which used to stand near the Town Hall. The timber framed building on the left is now occupied by Birmingham Midshires Building Society. Manchester House is just visible beyond.

Opposite and rather hidden by foliage is the Golden Cross, an old coaching inn which was rebuilt in 1932. The decorative details in the canopy and the big lights over the doors are typical of the period The first Golden Cross was probably in the Birmingham Midshires building.

High Street, Bromsgrove.

(83)

Parkside School, Bromsgrove.

40. Parkside School

The school was built on the north end of Bromsgrove Racecouse. With its solid doorway, warm brick walls and sandstone dressings, prominent quoins and perky bellcoat, it is one of those genial but dateless public buildings. This Queen Anne style was used freely for every type of building throughout the first forty odd years of the 20th century. It may be quite unoriginal, but it is sane and well mannered and sits comfortably in just about any town anywhere.

We hope you have enjoyed this ramble through the past and present streets of Bromsgrove. Prints of these pictures, framed or unframed, are available from Bill Hazlehurst's shop:

Memory Corner
The Picture Framing Gallery
Hagley Road
Hasbury
Hales Owen
B63 4QQ

0121 585 0506 (or at home 0121 550 3451)

You can also enquire at Mis Print, High Street, Bromsgrove.

Bill is available for commissions to draw private houses, churches and other historic buildings. He is planning other books of sketches and welcomes suggestions of buildings and scenes. Call at his shop and pass on your ideas and memories.